Table of Contents

Introduction to Recruitment 5

   1.1 What is Recruitment? 5

   1.2 Why Become a Recruiter?..5

The Role of a Recruiter..7

   2.1 Understanding the Importance of Talent Acquisition.......7

   2.2 The Evolving Role of Recruiters in the Modern World......8

Essential Skills and Qualifications for Recruiters........................9

   3.1 Interpersonal Skills of Communication, Empathy, and Active Listening 9

   3.2 Understanding Job Requirements and Candidate Fit......10

   3.3 Attracting Top Talent 10

   3.4 Leveraging Recruitment Tools.......................................11

   3.5 Staying Updated with Industry Trends...........................11

The Path to Becoming a Recruiter 13

   4.1 Education and Degree Choices......................................13

   4.2 Gaining Relevant Work Experience 14

   4.3 Certifications and Professional Development................14

The Recruitment Process 16

   5.1 Understanding the Hiring Needs: Collaboration with Hiring Managers..16

   5.2 Sourcing Strategies: Where to Find the Best Candidates 17

   5.3 Candidate Screening: Evaluating Resumes and Applications 17

   5.4 Conducting Interviews: Different Types and Techniques 18

5.5 Assessing Candidates: Testing and Reference Checks 19

5.6 Job Offer and Negotiation: Sealing the Deal 19

5.7 Onboarding: Setting the Stage for Success 20

A Day in the Life of a Recruiter 21

6.1 Morning Routine: Planning and Prioritization.................21

6.2 Sourcing Candidates...21

6.3 Screening and Interviewing: Candidate Assessment 22

6.4 Communication: Engaging with Candidates and Hiring Managers 22

6.5 Administrative Tasks: Documenting and Organizing 23

6.6 Continuous Learning: Staying Informed and Developing Skills 23

Pros and Cons of Being a Recruiter 25

7.1 Pros 25

7.2 Cons...26

7.3 Work-Life Balance 26

7.4 Overcoming Challenges...27

7.5 The Rewards of Being a Recruiter 27

Benefits and Salary Ranges for Recruiters 28

8.1 Benefits of Being a Recruiter...28

8.2 Salary Ranges for Recruiters 28

8.3 Additional Compensation Factors 29

8.4 Negotiating Compensation 30

Building a Successful Career in Recruitment............................32

9.1 Cultivating Core Competencies 32

9.2 Leveraging Technology and Data 33

9.3 Continuous Learning and Professional Development 33

9.4 Branding Yourself as a Recruiter 33

9.5 Building a Positive Candidate Experience 34

9.6 Balancing Quantity and Quality 34

Navigating Challenges in Recruitment 36

10.1 Challenge: Candidate Shortage and Competition 36

10.2 Challenge: Time Constraints and Urgency 37

10.3 Challenge: Managing Candidate Expectations and Rejections..37

10.4 Challenge: Overcoming Bias in Hiring 38

10.5 Challenge: Managing Client Expectations 38

10.6 Challenge: Professional Burnout...................................39

The Future of Recruitment: Embracing Innovation and Trends40

11.1 Leveraging Artificial Intelligence and Automation 40

11.2 Data-Driven Decision Making..41

11.3 Remote Work and Global Talent...................................41

11.4 Skill-Centric Recruitment 42

11.5 Building Virtual Talent Communities 42

11.6 Continuous Learning and Adaptation 43

Conclusion:..44

Chapter 1:

Introduction to Recruitment

1.1 What is Recruitment?

Recruitment is the process of identifying, attracting, and selecting qualified candidates to fill job vacancies within organizations. It plays a pivotal role in ensuring that companies have the right talent in place to achieve their business objectives. In essence, recruiters act as matchmakers, bridging the gap between job seekers and employers by finding the perfect fit for both parties.

The role of a recruiter involves much more than merely sifting through resumes. It requires a diverse skill set that encompasses interpersonal communication, marketing, sales, psychology, and the willingness to develop a keen understanding of the specific industry and job roles you are recruiting for. As a recruiter, you will play a crucial part in shaping the future of businesses and the careers of countless individuals.

1.2 Why Become a Recruiter?

Choosing a career in recruitment can be an immensely rewarding decision for several reasons:

1.2.1 Impacting Lives: As a recruiter, you have the power to influence and change lives. By helping job seekers find fulfilling careers and assisting companies in securing exceptional talent, you contribute to the growth and success of individuals and businesses.

1.2.2 Diverse Opportunities: The world of recruitment spans various industries and job functions, offering you the flexibility to specialize in areas that align with your passions and interests.

Whether it's IT, healthcare, finance, or any other field, there will always be a demand for skilled recruiters.

1.2.3 Financial Rewards: Recruiting can be a financially lucrative career, especially as you gain experience and expertise. Many recruitment roles offer commission-based incentives, which can significantly boost your earnings.

1.2.4 Fast-Paced and Dynamic: If you thrive in a dynamic environment where no two days are the same, recruitment could be an ideal fit. The constant interactions with candidates and clients, coupled with the urgency of filling positions, create an exciting and fast-paced work atmosphere.

1.2.5 Networking and Professional Development: Recruitment provides ample opportunities to network with industry professionals, build relationships, and expand your professional horizons. These connections can open doors to new opportunities and foster personal growth.

Chapter 2:

The Role of a Recruiter

2.1 Understanding the Importance of Talent Acquisition

Effective talent acquisition is a cornerstone of organizational success. A company's ability to attract, retain, and develop top talent directly impacts its competitiveness, innovation, and overall performance. Here are some key reasons why talent acquisition is crucial:

2.1.1 Driving Business Growth: Skilled and motivated employees are essential for driving business growth and achieving strategic objectives. An organization with a strong talent acquisition function can quickly respond to market demands by recruiting the right individuals to fill critical roles.

2.1.2 Enhancing Organizational Performance: Talent acquisition plays a vital role in ensuring that employees possess the necessary skills and expertise to excel in their roles. By recruiting high-performing individuals, organizations can enhance their overall performance and productivity.

2.1.3 Nurturing a Positive Company Culture: Recruiting individuals who align with the company's values and culture fosters a positive and cohesive work environment. A strong company culture enhances employee engagement and reduces turnover.

2.1.4 Building a Diverse Workforce: Diversity and inclusion are essential for fostering innovation and creativity within an organization. An effective talent acquisition strategy actively seeks candidates from diverse backgrounds and ensures equal opportunities for all.

2.1.5 Mitigating Recruitment Costs: Successful talent acquisition reduces the need for frequent recruitment cycles due to high employee retention rates. This helps organizations save both time and money that would otherwise be spent on repetitive hiring processes.

2.2 The Evolving Role of Recruiters in the Modern World

In the digital age, the role of a recruiter has evolved significantly. Advancements in technology, artificial intelligence, and data analytics have reshaped the recruitment landscape. Recruiters now have access to a wide array of tools and platforms that facilitate sourcing, screening, and candidate engagement.

However, despite the technological advancements, the human element remains essential in recruitment. Recruiters must cultivate strong interpersonal skills, empathy, and intuition to identify the right cultural fit and soft skills that algorithms may overlook. Moreover, with remote work becoming more prevalent, recruiters must adapt their strategies to engage with candidates from diverse geographical locations.

The modern recruiter must also stay abreast of industry trends, emerging job roles, and changes in the job market. A proactive approach to continuous learning and professional development is crucial for staying competitive and relevant in the rapidly evolving talent acquisition landscape.

As we proceed through this book, we will explore the core competencies and essential skills that recruiters need to succeed in the digital era. Understanding the role's foundation and its significance in an organization's success will lay the groundwork for building a fulfilling and impactful career in recruitment.

Chapter 3:

Essential Skills and Qualifications for Recruiters

In the competitive world of recruitment, possessing the right skills and qualifications is paramount to excel in the role. A successful recruiter is a versatile professional who demonstrates a unique blend of interpersonal, analytical, marketing, and technological abilities. In this chapter, we will explore the essential skills and qualifications that set recruiters apart and enable them to thrive in their careers.

3.1 Interpersonal Skills of Communication, Empathy, and Active Listening

3.1.1 Effective Communication: Communication lies at the heart of the recruiter's role. Recruiters must be adept at conveying job details, company information, and expectations clearly to candidates. Additionally, they need to establish open and transparent communication channels with hiring managers to understand their needs accurately.

3.1.2 Empathy and Emotional Intelligence: Successful recruiters display empathy and emotional intelligence when engaging with candidates. Understanding the emotions and perspectives of candidates during the recruitment process fosters positive experiences and establishes trust.

3.1.3 Active Listening: Active listening involves giving full attention to what candidates are saying, comprehending their responses, and asking relevant follow-up questions. Recruiters who actively listen can identify candidates' motivations and aspirations, leading to better candidate-job fit.

3.1.4 Relationship Building: Building and nurturing relationships with candidates, hiring managers, and industry professionals is essential for a recruiter's success. Strong relationships facilitate a steady pipeline of potential candidates and promote long-term partnerships with clients.

3.2 Understanding Job Requirements and Candidate Fit

3.2.1 Job Analysis and Market Research: Recruiters must possess analytical skills to conduct job analyses, which involve understanding the specific requirements of each role, industry trends, and salary benchmarks. This data-driven approach ensures that candidates are adequately matched with job positions.

3.2.2 Candidate Evaluation: Recruiters need to objectively assess candidates' qualifications, skills, and potential to succeed in a role. This involves asking the right questions, comparing candidates' experience and competencies against the job criteria, identifying potential red flags, and making data-informed decisions.

3.2.3 Problem-Solving: Recruitment often presents unique challenges, such as a shortage of suitable candidates or specific skill requirements. Effective recruiters are problem-solvers who can think creatively to overcome obstacles and find innovative solutions.

3.3 Attracting Top Talent

3.3.1 Employer Branding: Recruiters play a pivotal role in promoting their company's employer brand. Effectively communicating the company's values, culture, and opportunities enhances its appeal to top talent.

3.3.2 Candidate Engagement: Engaging candidates throughout the recruitment process involves using persuasive and personalized communication techniques. Recruiters need to maintain candidates' interest and enthusiasm for job opportunities.

3.3.3 Selling the Job Opportunity: Successful recruiters are skilled at selling a job opportunity to candidates by highlighting its unique benefits and growth potential. This requires understanding candidates' motivations and aligning them with the company's offerings.

3.4 Leveraging Recruitment Tools

3.4.1 Applicant Tracking Systems (ATS): Recruiters should be proficient in using ATS software to manage candidate databases, track hiring progress, and streamline administrative tasks.

3.4.2 Social Media and Networking Platforms: Social media platforms offer a vast pool of potential candidates. Recruiters need to be adept at leveraging platforms such as LinkedIn, Twitter, Tik Tok, and Facebook to source and engage with talent.

3.4.3 Video Interviewing and Virtual Communication: As remote work becomes more prevalent, recruiters must be comfortable with video interviewing tools and virtual communication platforms to conduct seamless interviews.

3.5 Staying Updated with Industry Trends

The world of recruitment is constantly evolving, with new technologies, sourcing methods, and candidate preferences emerging regularly. Recruiters must commit to continuous learning to stay updated with industry trends and best practices. Participating in workshops, attending conferences, listening to podcasts, following thought leaders on LinkedIn, and pursuing relevant certifications can enhance recruiters' skills and knowledge, making them more valuable to their organizations.

As you embark on your journey to become a recruiter, remember that possessing a diverse skill set is the key to success in the competitive talent acquisition landscape. Cultivating strong interpersonal skills, analytical abilities, marketing prowess, and technological acumen will position you as a proficient and sought-after recruiter. In the subsequent chapters, we will delve deeper into the educational and experiential pathways to become a recruiter, providing you with actionable steps to build a rewarding career in this exciting field.

Chapter 4:

The Path to Becoming a Recruiter

The journey to becoming a successful recruiter involves a combination of education, practical experience, and continuous learning. In this chapter, we will explore the various pathways that aspiring recruiters can pursue to enter and excel in the field of talent acquisition.

4.1 Education and Degree Choices

While there is no specific educational requirement to become a recruiter, having a relevant degree can provide a strong foundation for the role. The following are some degree choices that can be beneficial for aspiring recruiters:

4.1.1 Human Resources Management: A degree in Human Resources Management provides valuable insights into the recruitment process, talent acquisition strategies, and the legal aspects of hiring. It covers various HR functions, including training, compensation, and employee relations.

4.1.2 Psychology: A degree in Psychology offers an understanding of human behavior, motivations, and decision-making processes. This knowledge is invaluable when assessing candidate fit and managing candidate experiences during the recruitment process.

4.1.3 Business Administration: A degree in Business Administration equips aspiring recruiters with a broad understanding of organizational dynamics, strategic planning, and marketing principles. These skills are relevant when promoting the employer brand and selling job opportunities to candidates.

4.1.4 Communications or Marketing: Degrees in Communications or Marketing provide essential skills in effective communication, branding, and persuasive messaging. These skills are crucial in engaging candidates and showcasing the company's value proposition.

4.2 Gaining Relevant Work Experience

4.2.1 Internships and Entry-Level Positions: To kickstart a career in recruitment, consider internships or entry-level positions in HR departments or recruitment agencies. These opportunities offer hands-on experience in candidate sourcing, screening, and interviewing.

4.2.2 Customer Service or Sales Roles: Customer service and sales roles develop strong communication and persuasion skills, which are transferrable to recruitment. Experience in these roles showcases your ability to build relationships and engage with clients and candidates effectively.

4.2.3 Networking and Industry Involvement: Attend networking events, webinars, and industry conferences to connect with experienced recruiters and HR professionals. Engaging with the recruitment community can lead to valuable mentorship opportunities and insights into the field.

4.3 Certifications and Professional Development

4.3.1 Professional Certifications: Several organizations offer certifications specifically designed for recruiters. These certifications validate your expertise in recruitment best practices and can enhance your credibility as a recruiter. Some well-known certifications include:

- Certified Recruitment Professional (CRP)
- Certified Professional in Talent Development (CPTD)
- LinkedIn Recruiter Certification
- SHRM Talent Acquisition Specialty Credential

4.3.2 Professional Associations: Joining professional associations, such as the Society for Human Resource Management (SHRM) or the Association of Talent Acquisition Professionals (ATAP), provides access to valuable resources, training, and networking opportunities.

4.3.3 Continued Learning: The recruitment landscape evolves rapidly. To stay relevant and competitive, commit to continuous learning by reading industry publications, attending webinars, and enrolling in relevant courses.

4.3.4 Specializations: Consider pursuing specialized training in areas such as diversity and inclusion, executive search, or technical recruitment. Specializing in a niche can make you an expert in that domain and increase your marketability.

The path to becoming a recruiter is as diverse as the profession itself. Whether you choose to pursue a degree in Human Resources, gain experience through internships, or obtain certifications to demonstrate your expertise, each step will contribute to your growth as a recruiter.

Remember that becoming a successful recruiter is not solely about qualifications; it is also about passion, dedication, and the ability to connect with people. Embrace every opportunity to learn and grow, and don't be afraid to take on new challenges. As you progress in your journey, the skills and knowledge acquired will pave the way for a rewarding career in talent acquisition. In the following chapters, we will delve deeper into the recruitment process, providing you with valuable insights and practical tips to excel in each stage of the journey.

Chapter 5:

The Recruitment Process

The recruitment process is a multi-faceted and dynamic journey that involves various stages, each essential for finding and securing the right candidates. In this chapter, we will guide you through the step-by-step process of talent acquisition, from understanding hiring needs to making a successful job offer.

5.1 Collaboration with Hiring Managers to Understand Hiring Needs

The recruitment process begins with a thorough understanding of the hiring needs of the organization. Recruiters collaborate closely with hiring managers and department heads to gather comprehensive information about the vacant position. Key aspects to focus on during this stage include:

5.1.1 Job Description: Create and post a clear and detailed job description that outlines the key responsibilities, required qualifications, skills, experience necessary for the role, and company benefits. The job description serves as the foundation for evaluating candidates, and should draw candidates in to apply for the position and/or want to learn more about the company.

5.1.2 Cultural Fit: Understand the company's culture and values, as well as the team dynamics of the department seeking to fill the position. A candidate's cultural fit is crucial for fostering a positive work environment and enhancing team cohesion.

5.1.3 Cultural Fit: Understand the company's culture and values, as well as the team dynamics of the department seeking to fill the position. A candidate's cultural fit is crucial for fostering a positive work environment and enhancing team cohesion.

5.1.4 Hiring Timeline: Determine the desired timeline for the recruitment process, including the target date for the candidate to start in the position. This information helps in managing candidate expectations and streamlining the recruitment workflow.

5.2 Sourcing Strategies

Sourcing is the process of identifying potential candidates for a specific job opening. Effective sourcing strategies play a vital role in attracting a diverse pool of qualified candidates. Some common sourcing methods include:

5.2.1 Job Boards: Posting job advertisements on popular job boards, such as Indeed, Glassdoor, and LinkedIn, can reach a broad audience of active job seekers.

5.2.2 Social Media: Leverage social media platforms like LinkedIn, Twitter, and Facebook to showcase job opportunities and engage with potential candidates. Professional networking sites like LinkedIn are particularly valuable for sourcing candidates.

5.2.3 Employee Referrals: Encourage existing employees to refer potential candidates from their network. Employee referrals often lead to high-quality hires who align with the company's culture.

5.2.4 Talent Pipelining: Continuously build and maintain relationships with potential candidates who may be a fit for future positions. This proactive approach ensures a steady pipeline of qualified talent.

5.3 Evaluating Resumes and Applications

Candidate screening involves reviewing resumes, cover letters, and applications to shortlist candidates who meet the job requirements. Effective screening requires a keen eye for detail and the ability to identify key qualifications and experience. Consider the following during the screening process:

5.3.1 Keyword Analysis: Look for specific keywords and phrases that match the job description and indicate a candidate's relevant experience.

5.3.2 Core Competencies: Evaluate each candidate's core competencies and accomplishments to assess their suitability for the position.

5.3.3 Cultural Alignment: Assess whether the candidate's values and work style align with the company's culture and team dynamics.

5.4 Conducting Interviews

Interviewing is a critical stage of the recruitment process, providing an opportunity to assess candidates' skills, cultural fit, and potential fit within the organization. Different types of interviews can be conducted, such as:

5.4.1 Behavioral Interviews: These interviews focus on past experiences to gauge how candidates have handled specific situations in the past. The STAR (Situation, Task, Action, Result) method is often used to structure behavioral questions.

5.4.2 Competency-Based Interviews: These interviews assess candidates' skills and competencies required for the job. Recruiters ask questions that evaluate a candidate's ability to perform essential job functions.

5.4.3 Panel Interviews: Panel interviews involve multiple interviewers from different departments or levels within the organization. This approach provides a comprehensive assessment of the candidate from different perspectives.

5.4.4 Virtual Interviews: With remote work becoming prevalent, virtual interviews conducted via video conferencing platforms allow recruiters to connect with candidates worldwide.

5.5 Assessing Candidates

To make informed hiring decisions, additional assessments are often conducted to further evaluate candidates' qualifications and fit for the role:

5.5.1 Skills Assessments: Depending on the position, candidates may be required to complete skills tests, presentations, or sample projects to showcase their abilities.

5.5.2 Psychometric Testing: Psychometric assessments can provide insights into a candidate's personality traits, cognitive abilities, and work preferences.

5.5.3 Reference Checks: Contacting a candidate's references allows recruiters to verify the candidate's qualifications, work ethic, and performance in previous roles.

5.6 Job Offer and Negotiation

Once the ideal candidate is identified, extending a job offer is the next step. The job offer should be compelling and competitive to entice the candidate to accept the position. Some key considerations during this stage include:

5.6.1 Competitive Compensation: Offer a competitive salary and benefits package that aligns with industry standards and the candidate's experience.

5.6.2 Career Growth Opportunities: Highlight opportunities for career advancement and professional development within the organization.

5.6.3 Flexibility: If possible, be open to negotiating factors like remote work options or flexible work hours to accommodate the candidate's needs.

5.7 Onboarding and Setting the Stage for Success

Onboarding is a crucial phase that sets the foundation for the new hire's success within the organization. An effective onboarding process:

5.7.1 Welcomes the new employee into the company culture and fosters a sense of belonging.

5.7.2 Provides essential training and resources to ensure a smooth transition into the new role.

5.7.3 Introduces the new hire to their team and key stakeholders, fostering positive working relationships.

The recruitment process is a comprehensive journey that requires a strategic and methodical approach. Each stage plays a crucial role in ensuring that the right candidates are identified, engaged, and successfully integrated into the organization. In the next chapter, we will explore a day in the life of a recruiter, shedding light on the dynamic and rewarding aspects of this career.

Chapter 6:

A Day in the Life of a Recruiter

Recruiters lead fast-paced and dynamic professional lives, continuously juggling various tasks and responsibilities. In this chapter, we will provide a glimpse into a typical day in the life of a recruiter, highlighting the challenges and rewards that come with the job.

6.1 Planning and Prioritization

A recruiter's day often starts with a structured morning routine focused on planning and prioritization:

6.1.1 Reviewing the To-Do List: The day begins by reviewing the previous day's tasks and updating the to-do list for the current day. Recruiters prioritize their tasks based on urgency and importance.

6.1.2 Checking Emails and Messages: Recruiters respond to any urgent emails or messages received overnight. They also check for candidate responses, interview confirmations, and any new job requisitions.

6.1.3 Scheduling: Recruiters set aside time to schedule interviews, phone screens, and candidate assessments. Coordinating with candidates and hiring managers requires effective time management.

6.2 Sourcing Candidates

Recruiters use a variety of sources including Job Boards, Networking, Social Media to locate and communicate with candidates and potential candidates

An essential part of a recruiter's daily routine involves sourcing candidates to fill open positions:

6.2.1 Job Boards and Platforms: Recruiters post job openings on relevant job boards and platforms to attract applicants. They also search for potential candidates on these platforms.

6.2.2 Networking: Recruiters reach out to potential candidates through networking events, professional associations, and employee referrals.

6.2.3 Social Media: Recruiters engage with potential candidates on social media platforms like LinkedIn, responding to messages and comments.

6.3 Screening and Interviewing

As candidates apply and express interest, recruiters screen and interview them to evaluate their fit for the role:

6.3.1 Resume Review: Recruiters review resumes and applications, shortlisting candidates who meet the job criteria.

6.3.2 Phone Screens: Recruiters conduct initial phone screens to assess candidates' qualifications and motivations.

6.3.3 In-Person or Virtual Interviews: Qualified candidates are invited for in-person or virtual interviews, where recruiters assess their skills and cultural fit.

6.4 Engaging with Candidates and Hiring Managers

Throughout the day, recruiters engage in various forms of communication:

6.4.1 Candidate Follow-Ups: Recruiters keep candidates informed about the recruitment process, providing timely updates on their application status.

6.4.2 Feedback to Hiring Managers: Recruiters communicate interview feedback and candidate assessments to hiring managers, facilitating the decision-making process.

6.4.3 Client Meetings: Recruiters meet with clients to understand their hiring needs, provide progress reports, and discuss recruitment strategies.

6.5 Documenting and Organizing

Amidst all the candidate interactions and client meetings, recruiters must also manage administrative tasks:

6.5.1 Applicant Tracking System (ATS): Recruiters update candidate information and document interview notes in the ATS.

6.5.2 Compliance and Legal Requirements: Recruiters ensure compliance with hiring laws and regulations, such as equal opportunity employment guidelines. Experienced corporate Recruiters may even be responsible for providing training on hiring laws and best practices to company leaders.

6.5.3 Job Offer and Negotiation: When a candidate is selected, recruiters extend a job offer and manage the negotiation process.

6.6 Staying Informed and Developing Skills

A successful recruiter embraces continuous learning to stay informed about industry trends and enhance their skills:

6.6.1 Industry News: Recruiters dedicate time to read industry publications, blogs, and research reports to stay updated on market trends and changes.

6.6.2 Training and Workshops: Attending workshops and training sessions helps recruiters improve their sourcing, interviewing, and negotiation skills.

6.6.3 Networking Events: Recruiters participate in networking events to build connections and learn from experienced professionals.

6.7 Work-Life Balance: Managing Stress and Well-being

As the day comes to a close, recruiters prioritize their well-being and work-life balance:

6.7.1 Time Off and Rest: Recruiters understand the importance of unplugging and taking time off to recharge.

6.7.2 Stress Management: Managing stress is essential in a demanding profession. Recruiters adopt various strategies, such as exercise, mindfulness, and hobbies, to unwind and relax.

6.7.3 Celebrating Success: Recruiters celebrate successful placements and milestones, acknowledging their achievements and contributions.

A day in the life of a recruiter is dynamic, challenging, and fulfilling. From sourcing candidates to conducting interviews, and from engaging with clients to building relationships, recruiters play a crucial role in connecting talent with opportunities. The ability to manage multiple tasks, communicate effectively, and adapt to changing situations is key to thriving in this exciting career. In the following chapters, we will delve into the pros and cons of being a recruiter, providing a balanced perspective on the rewards and challenges of this profession.

Chapter 7:

Pros and Cons of Being a Recruiter

Becoming a recruiter offers a unique and rewarding career path, but like any profession, it comes with its own set of advantages and challenges. In this chapter, we will explore the pros and cons of being a recruiter, providing you with a balanced view of what to expect in this dynamic and impactful field.

7.1 Pros

7.1.1 Impacting Lives: As a recruiter, you have the power to influence and change lives. By connecting job seekers with fulfilling careers and helping companies secure exceptional talent, you play a crucial role in shaping individuals' futures and contributing to organizational success.

7.1.2 Diverse Opportunities: Recruitment spans across various industries and job functions, offering you the flexibility to specialize in areas that align with your passions and interests. Whether it's technology, healthcare, finance, or any other field, there will always be a demand for skilled recruiters.

7.1.3 Financial Rewards: Recruitment can be financially lucrative, especially as you gain experience and expertise. Many recruitment roles offer commission-based incentives, allowing you to significantly boost your earnings.

7.1.4 Fast-Paced and Dynamic: If you thrive in a dynamic environment where no two days are the same, recruitment is an ideal fit. The constant interactions with candidates and clients, coupled with the urgency of filling positions, create an exciting and fast-paced work atmosphere.

7.1.5 Networking and Professional Development: Recruitment provides ample opportunities to network with industry professionals, build relationships, and expand your professional horizons. These connections can open doors to new opportunities and foster personal growth.

7.2 Cons

7.2.1 Stress and Pressure: Meeting hiring targets and deadlines can be stressful. The pressure to find the right candidates quickly can sometimes lead to long working hours and tight timelines.

7.2.2 Rejection and Disappointment: Dealing with rejection is an inevitable part of recruitment. Not every candidate will be the perfect fit for a role, and not every job offer will be accepted. Managing candidate disappointment and client expectations can be challenging.

7.2.3 Competitive Market: The recruitment industry is competitive, with numerous agencies and independent recruiters vying for top talent. Standing out in the market and building a strong reputation requires consistent effort and a differentiated approach.

7.2.4 Administrative Burden: Recruiters must manage various administrative tasks, such as documentation, compliance, and data entry. Balancing these responsibilities with candidate engagement and sourcing can be time-consuming.

7.2.5 High Turnover: The recruitment industry itself experiences high turnover rates. As a recruiter, you may face turnover challenges both within your own organization and with candidates who change jobs frequently.

7.3 Work-Life Balance

Maintaining work-life balance is an ongoing challenge for recruiters, given the dynamic nature of the job and the need to be available during non-traditional working hours. However, many recruiters find ways to balance their personal and professional lives by setting boundaries, prioritizing self-care, and leveraging technology to streamline tasks.

7.4 Overcoming Challenges

As with any profession, challenges in recruitment can be overcome with determination and the right mindset. Here are some strategies for addressing the common challenges faced by recruiters:

7.4.1 Effective Time Management: Prioritize tasks, set realistic goals, and use productivity tools to manage your time efficiently.

7.4.2 Resilience and Adaptability: Embrace change and develop resilience to handle rejection and setbacks with a positive outlook.

7.4.3 Continuous Learning: Invest in professional development to stay updated with industry trends and best practices.

7.4.4 Team Collaboration: Foster a collaborative culture within your team to share knowledge and support each other.

7.5 The Rewards of Being a Recruiter

Despite the challenges, being a recruiter offers a fulfilling and impactful career. The satisfaction of matching the right candidate with the right job, witnessing the growth of individuals, and contributing to a company's success are rewarding aspects of this profession. Recruiters who thrive in this field are often passionate about people, dedicated to making a difference, and driven to succeed in a dynamic and ever-evolving industry.

In the subsequent chapters, we will explore the benefits and salary ranges for junior recruiters, experienced recruiters, and executive recruiters, helping you understand the financial aspects of this rewarding profession.

Chapter 8:

Benefits and Salary Ranges for Recruiters

Recruitment can be financially rewarding, and compensation often varies based on factors such as experience, industry, and geographical location. In this chapter, we will delve into the benefits of being a recruiter and provide general salary ranges for junior recruiters, experienced recruiters, and executive recruiters.

8.1 Benefits of Being a Recruiter

8.1.1 Competitive Compensation: Recruiters can earn a competitive base salary, and many recruitment roles offer performance-based incentives or commissions for successfully placing candidates.

8.1.2 Skill Development: Recruitment provides opportunities to develop a diverse skill set, including communication, negotiation, sales, and relationship building, which are transferrable to various career paths.

8.1.3 Networking Opportunities: Recruiters constantly interact with professionals from different industries, building a vast network that can lead to valuable connections and opportunities.

8.1.4 Career Progression: With experience and expertise, recruiters can advance into senior or leadership roles within their organization or even transition to other HR-related positions.

8.1.5 Job Satisfaction: Making successful placements and positively impacting candidates' lives can be highly rewarding and satisfying for recruiters.

8.2 Salary Ranges for Recruiters

It's important to note that salary ranges can vary significantly depending on factors such as the size of a company, location, industry, experience, and individual performance. The figures provided below are general estimates and may differ based on specific circumstances.

8.2.1 Junior Recruiters: Junior recruiters typically have less than two years of experience. Their base salary may range from $35,000 to $55,000 per year. As they gain experience and prove their abilities, their earnings can increase.

8.2.2 Recruiters (Mid-Level): Recruiters with two to five years of experience fall into the mid-level category. Their base salary ranges from $50,000 to $75,000 per year, with potential commission or performance-based bonuses.

8.2.3 Experienced Recruiters (Senior-Level): Recruiters with more than five years of experience and a track record of successful placements can earn a base salary ranging from $75,000 to $100,000 or more annually, along with higher commission opportunities.

8.2.4 Executive Recruiters: Executive recruiters, also known as headhunters, specialize in filling high-level executive positions. Their compensation can vary widely, with base salaries ranging from $100,000 to $150,000 or more, depending on their level of expertise and the complexity of the roles they handle.

8.3 Additional Compensation Factors

In addition to base salaries and commission-based incentives, recruiters may also enjoy other benefits and compensation factors, including:

8.3.1 Performance Bonuses: High-performing recruiters may receive additional performance-based bonuses tied to their individual or team achievements.

8.3.2 Health Benefits: Many companies provide comprehensive health and wellness benefits, including medical, dental, and vision coverage, to their employees.

8.3.3 Retirement Plans: Recruiters may have access to retirement savings plans, such as 401(k) or similar schemes, which help them save for the future.

8.3.4 Work Flexibility: Some recruiters enjoy flexible work arrangements, including remote work options or flexible hours, enabling them to maintain a better work-life balance.

8.3.5 Professional Development: Companies may support their recruiters' professional development by funding certifications, workshops, and industry conferences.

8.4 Negotiating Compensation

When entering a recruitment role or seeking career advancement, it's essential to negotiate compensation effectively. Consider the following tips when negotiating your salary and benefits:

8.4.1 Research Market Rates: Research industry salary benchmarks and the average compensation for recruiters in your region to have a realistic understanding of your worth.

8.4.2 Highlight Achievements: Emphasize your past successes and contributions to showcase your value to the organization.

8.4.3 Discuss Performance Metrics: If applicable, discuss how you can contribute to the company's growth and suggest tying your compensation to specific performance metrics.

8.4.4 Consider the Entire Package: Evaluate the overall benefits package, including bonuses, health benefits, retirement plans, and work flexibility, as these can significantly impact your total compensation.

Remember that salary negotiation is a collaborative process. Be professional, confident, and prepared during the negotiation, and aim to reach a mutually beneficial agreement.

Being a recruiter offers numerous benefits, including competitive compensation, skill development, and networking opportunities. While salaries can vary based on experience and specialization, recruitment is a financially rewarding career path with ample opportunities for career growth and job satisfaction. As you progress in your career, continuous learning and consistently delivering exceptional results will position you for success and advancement within the dynamic and fulfilling world of talent acquisition.

Chapter 9:

Building a Successful Career in Recruitment

Building a successful career in recruitment requires a combination of skills, dedication, and a strategic approach. In this chapter, we will provide you with valuable insights and practical tips to help you excel in the field of talent acquisition and achieve your professional goals.

9.1 Cultivating Core Competencies

9.1.1 Communication Skills: Effective communication is at the heart of recruitment. Practice active listening, articulate your thoughts clearly, and tailor your messaging to resonate with candidates and clients.

9.1.2 Relationship Building: Nurture relationships with candidates, hiring managers, and industry professionals. Strong professional relationships lead to a broader network and potential future opportunities.

9.1.3 Adaptability: Recruitment is a dynamic field, and adaptability is crucial to thrive amidst changes in the job market, industry trends, organizational complexities, and candidate preferences.

9.1.4 Problem-Solving Abilities: Develop strong problem-solving skills to navigate challenges, overcome obstacles, and find innovative solutions in the recruitment process.

9.1.5 Emotional Intelligence: Demonstrate empathy and emotional intelligence when engaging with candidates. Understanding their motivations and concerns fosters positive candidate experiences.

9.2 Leveraging Technology and Data

9.2.1 Embrace ATS: Familiarize yourself with Applicant Tracking Systems (ATS) to streamline candidate management and enhance the efficiency of the recruitment process.

9.2.2 Data-Driven Approach: Utilize data analytics to identify trends, optimize sourcing strategies, and make informed decisions during candidate selection.

9.2.3 Automation Tools: Embrace automation tools for repetitive tasks, allowing you to focus on relationship-building and strategic aspects of recruitment.

9.3 Continuous Learning and Professional Development

9.3.1 Stay Informed: Keep yourself updated with the latest industry trends, best practices, and technological advancements through reading, webinars, and industry events.

9.3.2 Pursue Certifications: Consider earning professional certifications in recruitment and related fields to enhance your credibility and expertise.

9.3.3 Seek Mentorship: Connect with experienced recruiters or mentors who can provide guidance and insights into the profession.

9.3.4 Attend Conferences: Participate in industry conferences to network with peers, learn from experts, and gain exposure to emerging recruitment trends.

9.4 Branding Yourself as a Recruiter

9.4.1 Online Presence: Create a strong online presence, particularly on professional networking platforms like LinkedIn, to showcase your expertise and connect with potential candidates and clients.

9.4.2 Personal Branding: Develop a personal brand that reflects your values, strengths, and unique selling points as a recruiter.

9.4.3 Thought Leadership: Share your knowledge and expertise through writing blogs, articles, or contributing to industry publications. Establishing yourself as a thought leader elevates your professional reputation.

9.5 Building a Positive Candidate Experience

9.5.1 Timely Communication: Maintain open and transparent communication with candidates throughout the recruitment process, keeping them informed about their application status.

9.5.2 Respect and Empathy: Treat candidates with respect and empathy, regardless of the outcome. Providing constructive feedback can leave a lasting positive impression.

9.5.3 Onboarding Support: Extend your support during the onboarding process to ensure a smooth transition for the newly hired candidates.

9.6 Balancing Quantity and Quality

Recruiters often face pressure to fill positions quickly, but it's essential to strike a balance between quantity and quality:

9.6.1 Focus on Fit: Prioritize finding candidates who align with the company's culture and values rather than solely focusing on quick placements.

9.6.2 Build Talent Pipelines: Invest time in building a talent pipeline to have a pool of potential candidates ready for future opportunities.

9.6.3 Manage Workload: Strategically manage your workload and set realistic expectations with clients and hiring managers to maintain the quality of the recruitment process.

By cultivating core competencies, leveraging technology, pursuing continuous learning, and building a positive brand, you can position yourself for a successful and fulfilling career in recruitment. Remember that success in this field comes from a combination of hard work, dedication, and a genuine passion for connecting talent with opportunities. As you progress in your journey, embrace challenges as opportunities for growth and continuously seek ways to improve and excel in your role as a recruiter.

Chapter 10:

Navigating Challenges in Recruitment

While a career in recruitment offers numerous rewards, it also comes with its fair share of challenges. In this chapter, we will explore common challenges faced by recruiters and provide strategies to navigate them effectively, ensuring continued success in the dynamic world of talent acquisition.

10.1 Candidate Shortage and Competition

One of the most significant challenges recruiters encounter is the scarcity of qualified candidates, particularly in niche industries or for specialized roles. Additionally, recruiters often compete with other organizations and agencies for the same talent.

Navigating the Challenge:

- Expand Sourcing Channels: Diversify your sourcing strategies by exploring new channels, attending industry events, and engaging in social media recruitment to reach untapped talent pools.

- Talent Pipelining: Proactively build and maintain relationships with potential candidates and employees to create a talent pipeline, allowing you to quickly access suitable candidates when job openings arise.

- Employer Branding: Enhance your company's employer brand to attract top talent. Showcase the organization's unique culture, values, and opportunities to differentiate it from competitors.

10.2 Time Constraints and Urgency

Recruiters often face time-sensitive hiring demands from hiring managers, leading to tight deadlines and high-pressure situations.

Navigating the Challenge:

- Efficient Scheduling: Utilize scheduling tools to streamline the interview process and optimize your time management.

- Set Realistic Expectations: Communicate openly with hiring managers about the time required for each stage of the recruitment process, setting realistic expectations.

- Prioritize: Focus on high-priority roles and manage your workload effectively. Delegate tasks when possible and collaborate with team members to share responsibilities.

10.3 Managing Candidate Expectations and Rejections

Rejection is a natural part of the recruitment process, and managing candidate expectations and emotions requires sensitivity and empathy.

Navigating the Challenge:

- Transparent Communication: Maintain open and honest communication with candidates, providing timely feedback and updates on their application status.

- Constructive Feedback: Offer constructive feedback to candidates who are not selected, highlighting areas for improvement while maintaining a positive tone.

- Candidate Experience: Prioritize candidate experience throughout the recruitment journey, ensuring that candidates feel valued and respected, regardless of the outcome.

10.4 Overcoming Bias in Hiring

Recruiters must be vigilant about unconscious bias in the recruitment process, ensuring that all candidates are evaluated based on their qualifications and potential.

Navigating the Challenge:

- Diversity and Inclusion: Promote diversity and inclusion within the organization and during the recruitment process. Advocate for diverse candidate slates and foster an inclusive hiring culture.

- Standardized Assessment: Implement standardized interview questions and evaluation criteria to minimize the impact of bias and ensure fairness in candidate assessments.

- Training and Awareness: Provide training and guidance to recruiters and hiring managers on identifying and addressing unconscious bias in hiring decisions.

10.5 Managing Client Expectations

Recruiters must navigate the expectations of clients and hiring managers while balancing the reality of the job market and candidate availability.

Navigating the Challenge:

- Educate Clients: Provide insights into the current job market, salary trends, and candidate availability to set realistic expectations with clients.

- Regular Updates: Maintain open lines of communication with clients, providing regular updates on the progress of the recruitment process.

- Align Expectations: Align with clients on job requirements, cultural fit, and salary ranges to ensure a smoother recruitment journey.

10.6 Professional Burnout

Recruitment can be demanding and fast-paced, leading to potential burnout if not managed effectively.

Navigating the Challenge:

- Set Boundaries: Establish boundaries between work and personal life to avoid overworking and burnout. Allocate time for hobbies, exercise, and relaxation.
- Seek Support: Lean on colleagues and mentors for support and guidance during challenging times.
- Time Off: Utilize vacation days and take breaks when needed to recharge and rejuvenate.

By proactively addressing these challenges and implementing effective strategies, recruiters can navigate the complexities of the talent acquisition landscape more efficiently. Recognize that challenges are opportunities for growth, and maintaining a positive attitude and resilience will contribute to your long-term success in the rewarding field of recruitment.

Chapter 11:

The Future of Recruitment: Embracing Innovation and Trends

The recruitment landscape is continuously evolving, driven by technological advancements, changing candidate preferences, and shifts in the job market. In this final chapter, we will explore the future of recruitment, highlighting emerging trends and innovations that recruiters must embrace to stay relevant and successful in the years to come.

11.1 Leveraging Artificial Intelligence and Automation

Artificial Intelligence (AI) and automation are revolutionizing the recruitment process, streamlining repetitive tasks, and enhancing efficiency. Recruiters can leverage AI-powered tools for:

- Resume Screening: AI algorithms can analyze resumes and applications, shortlisting candidates based on their qualifications and experience, saving time and effort.

- Candidate Matching: AI-driven candidate matching systems can assess a candidate's skills and cultural fit, ensuring a more accurate and unbiased candidate assessment.

- Chatbots and Virtual Assistants: AI-powered chatbots can engage with candidates, answering frequently asked questions and providing a seamless candidate experience.

Embracing AI and automation allows recruiters to focus on building meaningful relationships with candidates and clients, while technology handles time-consuming administrative tasks.

11.2 Data-Driven Decision Making

Data analytics and predictive modeling are becoming essential tools for recruiters. By analyzing vast amounts of data, recruiters can make informed decisions on sourcing strategies, candidate assessments, and market trends.

Data-driven recruitment enables:

- Identifying Skill Gaps: Analyzing industry trends and skill demand allows recruiters to anticipate future talent needs and plan talent acquisition accordingly.

- Improving Candidate Experience: Analyzing candidate feedback and engagement data helps optimize the recruitment process, enhancing the candidate experience.

- Enhancing Diversity and Inclusion: Data analysis can highlight potential bias in hiring practices and enable recruiters to implement more inclusive hiring strategies.

11.3 Remote Work and Global Talent

The rise of remote work and virtual collaboration has expanded the potential talent pool for recruiters. Organizations are increasingly open to hiring remote employees, allowing recruiters to source candidates from around the world.

Recruiters must adapt to:

- Virtual Hiring: Conducting interviews and onboarding processes through video conferencing platforms to accommodate remote candidates.

- Cross-Cultural Competence: Understanding cultural differences and preferences to effectively engage with candidates from diverse backgrounds.

- Time Zone Management: Coordinating interviews and communications across different time zones for global recruitment.

11.4 Skill-Centric Recruitment

The job market is evolving rapidly, with an increasing emphasis on skills over traditional qualifications. Skill-centric recruitment focuses on identifying candidates with the right capabilities and potential to learn and adapt to changing job requirements.

To embrace skill-centric recruitment:

- Redefine Job Descriptions: Focus on skills and competencies required for the role rather than specific academic qualifications.

- Upskilling and Reskilling: Encourage continuous learning and support candidates and employees in acquiring new skills.

- Emphasize Transferable Skills: Look for transferable skills that candidates can bring from other industries or roles, enabling diverse talent acquisition.

11.5 Building Virtual Talent Communities

Talent communities are networks of potential candidates who may not be actively seeking jobs but are interested in future opportunities. Virtual talent communities allow recruiters to maintain connections with potential candidates and engage them through content, webinars, and newsletters.

Benefits of virtual talent communities include:

- Talent Pipelining: Proactively build relationships with potential candidates, ensuring access to a pool of qualified talent when vacancies arise.

- Enhanced Employer Branding: Regular engagement with candidates through virtual communities strengthens the organization's employer brand.

- Faster Hiring: Virtual talent communities allow recruiters to identify suitable candidates quickly, expediting the recruitment process.

11.6 Continuous Learning and Adaptation

The future of recruitment is dynamic and unpredictable. As new technologies and trends emerge, recruiters must remain agile and adaptable to stay ahead.

Key strategies for continuous learning and adaptation:

- Attend Industry Events: Participate in recruitment conferences, webinars, and workshops to stay updated with the latest industry developments.

- Networking: Engage with peers and industry professionals to learn from their experiences and share best practices.

- Embrace Change: Be open to experimenting with new tools and strategies, embracing innovation as it arises.

Conclusion

The future of recruitment is exciting and full of possibilities. By embracing technological innovations, leveraging data-driven insights, and adapting to evolving trends, recruiters can thrive in this dynamic landscape.

Remember that at the core of recruitment is the human element - building meaningful connections with candidates and clients, understanding their needs, and helping them find the perfect fit. As you embark on the journey into the future of recruitment, hold on to the values of empathy, integrity, and excellence that make the profession impactful and rewarding.

With an unwavering commitment to continuous learning, innovative practices, and a genuine passion for connecting talent with opportunities, you will not only succeed in the future of recruitment but also contribute to the growth and success of organizations and individuals alike.

Throughout this book, we've explored the multifaceted world of recruitment, from understanding the process to building a successful career as a recruiter. We've discussed the essential skills, qualifications, and day-to-day responsibilities of recruiters, as well as the pros and cons of the profession.

As you embark on your journey as a recruiter or continue to grow in your recruitment career, remember that success in this field requires a combination of technical expertise, interpersonal skills, and continuous learning. Embrace challenges as opportunities for growth, and consistently strive to provide exceptional experiences for both candidates and clients.

Whether you choose to specialize in executive search, technical recruitment, or any other area within talent acquisition, your role as a recruiter will have a significant impact on shaping individuals' careers and contributing to the success of organizations.

Always approach recruitment with empathy, integrity, and a genuine passion for connecting talent with opportunities. By doing so, you will not only build a rewarding career but also leave a positive and lasting impact on the lives of those you serve.

Best of luck on your journey as a recruiter, and may your dedication and expertise lead you to a fulfilling and successful career in the exciting world of talent acquisition.

Wishing you a successful and fulfilling career as a recruiter in the ever-evolving world of talent acquisition!

www.ingramcontent.com/pod-product-compliance
Lightning Source LLC
Chambersburg PA
CBHW070959240526
45469CB00017B/2482